Creepy Crawly
Calypso

For Mercedes, who counts — T. L.

For Matthew — D. H.

Barefoot Books
124 Walcot Street
Bath
BA1 5BG

First published in Great Britain in 2004 by Barefoot Books Ltd
This paperback edition printed in 2004

This book was typeset in Mercurius Medium
The illustrations were prepared in watercolour,
pen and ink, and crayon on thick watercolour paper

Graphic design by Barefoot Books, Bath
Colour separation by Grafiscan, Verona
Printed and bound in Singapore by Tien Wah Press Pte Ltd

This book has been printed on 100% acid-free paper

ISBN 1 84148 138 6

British Library Cataloguing-in-Publication Data: a catalogue
record for this book is available from the British Library

3 5 7 9 8 6 4 2

Creepy Crawly
Calypso

written by **Tony Langham**

illustrated by **Debbie Harter**

Barefoot Books
Celebrating Art and Story

If you like good music,
if you want a treat,
just hear these creepy crawlies
play their cool calypso beat!

1 First comes the spider,
banging steel drums.

2 Second come the butterflies,
with accordions.

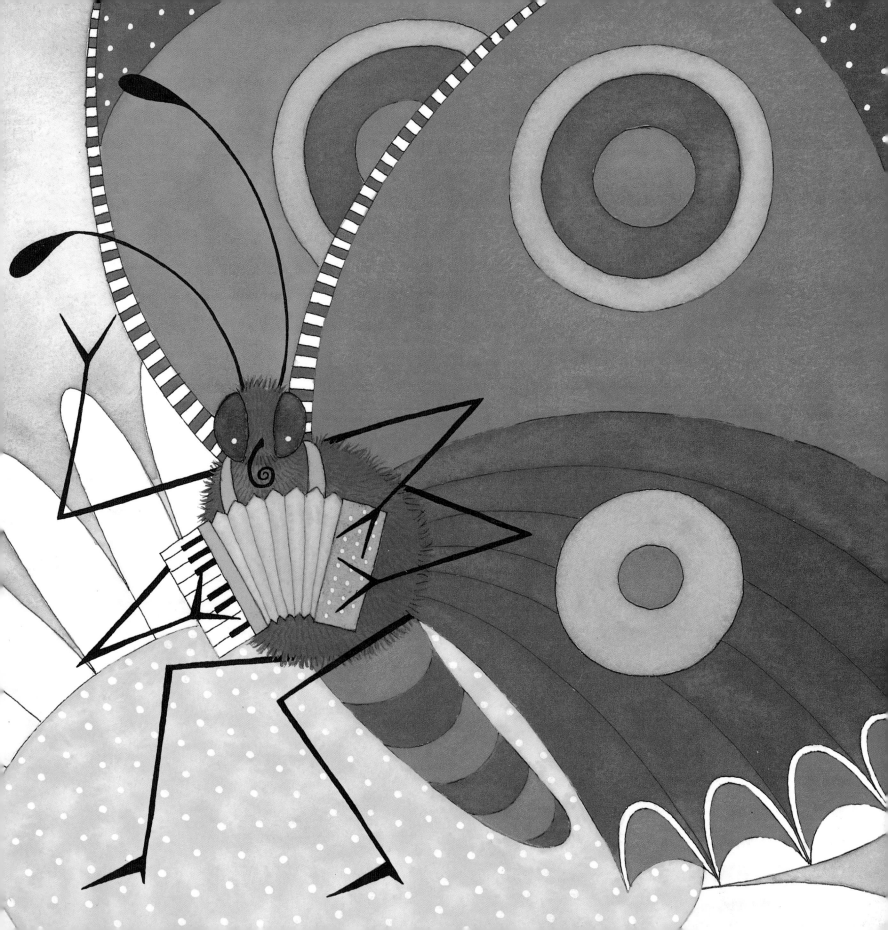

3 Third come the cockroaches, playing saxophones.

4 **Fourth come the dragonflies,
blowing their trombones.**

5 Fifth come the fireflies,
with brass trumpets to toot.